Anatomy of Yang Family Tai Chi

A Guide for Teachers and Students

by Steffan de Graffenried

Translation of Original Chinese Texts

by Fei Lincoln

Anatomy of Yang Family Tai Chi
A Guide for Teachers and Students
© 2007 Steffan de Graffenried

Library of Congress Control Number: 2008900683

ISBN 978-0-9798956-2-3

2.0

Nomentira Publications
http://www.nomentira.com
nomentirapublications@gmail.com

Appreciation

First and foremost I give constant thanks to Almighty God for bringing wonderful teachers into my life and for giving me the ability to grasp all of these concepts so that I could write this book. I would also like to thank my mother for all the sacrifices she made in order that I might study martial arts from an early age. I give thanks to Master Jamie Hooper, my first real kung fu sifu, to whom I owe a great debt for the immense amount of knowledge I pulled from his head. I thank Grandmaster Doc-Fai Wong for his brilliant teaching methodology, his intricately detailed correction of my postures and his incredible example of what perfection in motion should look like. I would like to thank my yoga teacher, Bruce Bowditch, for helping me to understand that the principles and concepts in this book extend far beyond Tai Chi to virtually every physical practice and therefore deepening my own comprehension...deep calls to deep. Special thanks to Dr. Jon Alan Smith, D.C. for his patience with my constant quizzing about anatomy and kinesiology. Thanks to Fei Lincoln for her beautiful translations of the original Tai Chi Classic texts. Last but by no means least, I thank my beautiful wife Starr for her never ending patience and valuable editing skills...she is my all.

Table of Contents

Table of Contents (cont.)

Tai Chi Chuan Lineage

太極師乘表

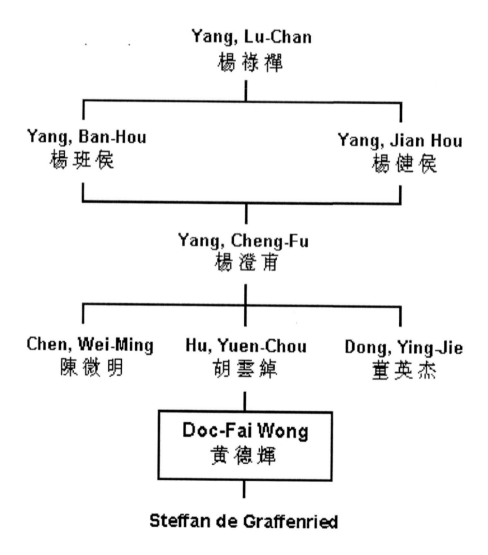

Yang, Lu-Chan
楊祿禪

Yang, Ban-Hou
楊班侯

Yang, Jian Hou
楊健侯

Yang, Cheng-Fu
楊澄甫

Chen, Wei-Ming
陳微明

Hu, Yuen-Chou
胡雲緯

Dong, Ying-Jie
董英杰

Doc-Fai Wong
黃德輝

Steffan de Graffenried

Preface

Tai Chi Chuan has been practiced, taught, used for defense and passed down through many generations. In my lineage I am the 6th generation from Yang Lu-Chan, founder of Yang Family Tai Chi Chuan. This art was passed to me in the traditional way, through physical and oral instruction and through the study of the classic writings of Tai Chi Chuan (the Tai Chi Classics). Through years of cross-referencing different translations of the same texts, directly studying the Chinese texts and incessantly quizzing my sifu, I began to understand the true meaning behind all of the flowery, esoteric and mysterious language that has confounded western practitioners for years. As with any practice of physical movement, there are varying schools of thought. If during the study of this book you encounter something that your particular school of Tai Chi disagrees with, then I would ask you to try it and let it stand up to the test of the Eight Stabilities. I think you will find that my axioms are sound and my points are clear.

In the Tai Chi Classics it says, "...first you must learn the feet and inches and then the hundredth parts and thousandth parts." Here in the west the hundredth parts and thousandth parts have eluded us either because of ignorance, language barriers or because there are some Chinese teachers who have held back the high level Tai Chi principles from westerners. Fortunately, my own sifu desires to spread the true principles of Tai Chi to the world. In this book, it is my intention to shed light on the complexities of Tai Chi which have only been alluded to in the classic texts and to give students and teachers a clear, concise methodology for moving from the beginner level to enlightenment. Make no mistake - this is not a "learn Tai Chi in a day" quick fix guide. You cannot skip past the feet and inches. You cannot start at the 36th chamber. Applying the principles in this book may or may not shorten your Tai Chi journey, but at least you will have a clear view of where you are going and how you will get there. You will be able to test your progress with the Eight Stabilities test and even test your Qi development with a simple muscle test. I urge you to take this journey one step at a time ... day by day. Do not be in a hurry or you may miss a turn and be a thousand miles off course before you realize it. I urge you as well that if you are reading this book and are not studying directly from a Tai Chi teacher (sifu), then put this book down and find a local Tai Chi class and begin lessons before returning to this book. I most certainy do not mean for this book to replace a flesh and blood teacher nor do I mean for this book to replace actual study of the classic texts. Practice and study ... practice and study ... practice and study! It is by this method that you will reach your first goal in Tai Chi: achieving conscious movement. Whether you are beginner or advanced, have been studying for one month or ten years, I believe you will find this book both enlightening and challenging.

Section One

What Is
Tai Chi Chuan?

Grandmaster Doc-Fai Wong

What Is Tai Chi Chuan?

What Is Tai Chi Chuan?

From the time Tai Chi Chuan arrived on western soil there has been misinformation, misunderstanding and confusion about the meaning of the words *Tai ... Chi ... Chuan.* Of course, we pulled out our trusty Chinese-English dictionary and looked up each word. *Supreme ... Ultimate ... Fist ...* WOW! That sounds fantastic! It sounds so great, in fact, that many Tai Chi practitioners become offended when told that this is not the true translation. The true meaning hinges on the first two words (*tai* and *chi*) but not on the individual translation of these words. The Chinese ideograms have a special meaning when placed together. "Tai Chi" refers to the origins of the universe, the beginning and ending of all things. In the west we think of time as a very linear entity as though the beginning and ending are separate and a great distance apart. In the east, however, time is thought of as circular so that when one gets to the end of it, then he is back at the beginning again. So "Tai Chi" the "supreme" or "great ending" also refers to the "great beginning." Tai Chi is, according to Taoist thinking, what birthed the universe. The Treatise on Tai Chi Chuan states that Tai Chi is the mother of Yin and Yang. This means that before Yin and Yang were separate entities that they existed together in perfect harmony. The symbol that westerners refer to as the "yin yang" is actually called the "Tai Chi" symbol.

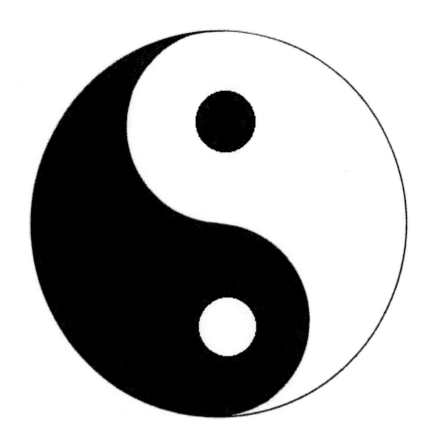

The Tai Chi symbol (Tai Chi Tu 太極圖) represents Yin and Yang as one - in harmonious balance as they were in the beginning. You should summize from all of this that *Tai Chi Chuan* means the fighting style (fist) based on what the Tai Chi symbol represents: male and female, hard carrying soft and soft carrying hard, and the opposing forces of the universe functioning in perfect harmony. It has become a fitting symbol for a fighting style so beautifully complex that it takes a page and a half to explain the meaning of its name.

Tai Chi Has Two Goals

Sun Tzu in the *Art of War* said, "In ancient times men first made themselves invincible and then learned the ways of strategy."

Ultimately you have only two goals in Tai Chi. The first is achieving conscious movement and the second is attaining to the level of interpreting energy. Both are very lofty goals indeed.

Achieving conscious movement means that you have eliminated all unconscious movement. You have mastered yourself. You have become completely self-aware. You do this by practicing the form and applying all of the concepts in this book. Fu Zhong-Wen, while quoting Li I-Yu, said that practicing the form is the *Kung Fu* of knowing yourself and pushing hands is the *Kung Fu* of knowing others. This will not happen in a month's time.

Attaining to the level of interpreting energy has to do with mastering others through pushing hands. This cannot be truly achieved until you have mastered yourself. You will not be able to fully concentrate on interpreting the energy of your opponent while you are attempting to maintain your own balance.

Having mastered these two things, you will be what the classics call a "peerless boxer" - a fighter without equal.

Ch'ien
Heaven, Sky

Sun
Wind, Wood

Tui
Lake, Mist

K'an
Water, Moon

Li
Fire, Sun

Ken
Mountain

Chen
Thunder

K'un
Earth

Liu He Ba Gua Wu Bu

The Six Harmonies

Eight Gates & Five Steps

The Six Harmonies are divided into three external harmonies and three internal harmonies. The external harmonies are the most important for beginners and the internal harmonies should be taught to your more advanced students.

The Three External Harmonies (San Wai He) Are:

1. Hands and feet in harmony

2. Elbows and knees in harmony

3. Shoulders and waist (hips) in harmony

The Three Internal Harmonies (San Nei He) Are:

1. The Yi (intention) and the Shen (spirit, awareness) in harmony

2. The Yi and the Qi (internal energy) in harmony

3. The Qi and the Jing (intrinsic or organic energy) in harmony

External harmony can only occur when there is motion. The hands and feet in harmony means that when the front foot steps in a particular direction or turns inwardly or outwardly that the front hand moves in a similar way.

After the feet are planted (soles of the feet flat on the ground) then we can only talk about the elbows and knees and shoulders and waist being in harmony.

The elbows and knees move forward together, backward together, and turn from one side to the other in unison. Not only this, but they also end in the same vertical line unless the hips are squared forward with both hands at or past the front knee.

The shoulders and waist remain in harmony by always turning in the same direction and with the same energy even though they may not end up vertically plumb to one another.

Teacher's Notes:

Hands and feet are easiest to keep harmonious when they are both moving in toward the centerline as in the transition between left and right brush knee.

The three external harmonies can olny be truly realized through the mastery of the three internal harmonies.

The harmony of the Yi and Shen is the easiest for the beginner to grasp. This concept has been discussed in every major historical text about war, fighting and strategy. It is the harmony of your intention and your awareness. It is the ability to focus on one opponent but also to be acutely aware of other potential opponents around you.

Musashi in his *Go Rin No Sho* called it "developing the two-fold gaze of perception and sight." This ability reaches far beyond a simple one- on-one confrontation to large scale battle and even into everyday life. This is the ability to focus on the present moment but also to be aware of how your actions may affect the big picture of your life.

The harmony of the Yi and the Qi is the action of allowing your Qi (internal energy) to be directed and carried by your Yi (will or intention). Of course, you must have already developed the ability to direct your Qi in a given direction...no easy feat. Also, the Qi must have already sunken to the Dan Tien in order for it to be directed at or into an opponent.

The harmony of the Qi and the Jing is your ability to direct your Qi along the same path as your Jing (intrinsic energy). Intrinsic energy comprises the Li (muscular strength) and the integrity of the Chuan Jia (fighting frame). This is the perfect structural alignment of your tendons and bones. The harmony of the Qi and the Jing can only be accomplished when you are using the mind and not force to create the Chuan Jia.

Shen is created by this state of harmony between the Yi and the Qi and the Qi and the Jing. When all of these things are harmonious we say that the Shen is High or lifted.

The Eight Gates Are:

Ward-Off (Peng), North, Kuan

Roll-Back (Lu), South, Li

Press (Ji), East, Zhen

Push (An), West, Dui

Pull-Down (Tsai or Cai), Northwest, Qian

Split (Lieh or Lie), Southwest, Kun

Elbow-Stroke (Chou or Zhou), Northeast, Gen

Shoulder-Stroke (Kao), Southeast, Xun

The Five Steps Are:

Advance Step (Jin Bu), North, Water

Retreat Step (Tui Bu), South, Fire

Left-side Gazing (Zou Gu), East, Wood

Right-side Looking (You Pan), West, Metal

Central Earth (Zhong Ding), Earth

The Eight Gates and Five Steps comprise the Thirteen Postures of Tai Chi Chuan (Shi San Shi). The Eight Gates are the four sides and the four corners and correspond to the eight trigrams of the I-Ching. The Five Steps are directly related to the Five Elements; metal, wood, water, fire and earth.

Jin Bu means advancing forward or to close in on the opponent. Jin Bu is related to the direction North and corresponds to the element Water. Water floods in very powerfully and yet is soft and yielding when still.

Tui Bu means withdrawing the body away from the opponent but not separating from him. Tui Bu is related to the direction South which corresponds to the Fire element. This denotes how you retreat while attacking as you see in the posture Step Back and Repulse the Monkey.

Zuo Gu means to move diagonally to the left. Gazing means being watchful and careful. Moving diagonally to the left means that you are trying to gain an advantage by being at your opponent's right shoulder. Also, moving in this direction allows you to protect your right side. Zou Gu is related to the direction East and the element Wood.

You Pan means shift your body sideways. *You* (右) means right and *Pan* is looking forward. So you are able to quickly shift the body sideways in order to avoid attack. *You Pan* is related to the direction West and the element Metal.

Zhong Ding is the central earth and means to keep yourself balanced and stable. This corresponds to the concept of "stand like a balance and turn like a wheel."

Qi

How do I know?

Many students begin their study of Tai Chi with the intention of developing internal power or *Qi* (pronounced "chee"). There is nothing wrong with this idea as long as you, as a student, understand that it is and always will be the physical practice which is responsible for any and all Qi development. It is the correct physical practice which allows the natural Qi to sink into the Dan Tien. It is the physical practice which produces greater and greater levels of Qi. It is the physical practice that teaches you how to direct and emit that Qi from your body into the body of your opponent.

How do you know if, in fact, your Qi has sunk into the Dan Tien? How can you tell how much Qi you have and if you are yet able to emit it?

I will present here a simple test for ascertaining your level of Qi development. You will need a willing partner for this test. A beginner student or untrained person is best for your first few attempts. This is because you want someone with obviously weaker Qi development than you so that you will be able to ascertain development in the slightest level.

Have your partner stand in front of you and extend his arm out toward you with his fist level with his shoulder. Have him hold strong in that position while you apply some pressure downward to his fist. Do not press down harder than your partner can hold. After this brief initial gauging test, clear your mind and focus angry energy toward your partner and press downward on his fist again with exactly the same amount of force as you used during your initial test. If your partner's arm weakens and you are able to press it down, then you know that you are able to emit your Qi. I have you use angry energy because it is the easiest negative energy to emit. As you develop your Qi more you will be able to weaken your partner more and more. Eventually you will be able to weaken your partner without touching him (using a third partner to apply pressure to the arm for the test). You should be able to move further away from your partner as your development continues to augment.

It is important to note here that your partner should maintain a calm, natural expression on his face so as not to interfere with the test. As your study and training continue you will need to perform this test using positive energy or positive intention (Yi). In the case of the emission of positive energy, you will find that your partner's arm will grow stronger instead of weaker. There is only one Qi and this Qi is augmented and carried on your intention. Whether that intention is negative or positive determines what the Qi does to your partner. Negative intention (i.e. bad thoughts, sadness, anger or just a pessimistic attitude) weakens your partner and even people standing near you. Positive intention (i.e. thoughts of love, happiness, joy or an optimistic attitude) strengthens your partner and those around you.

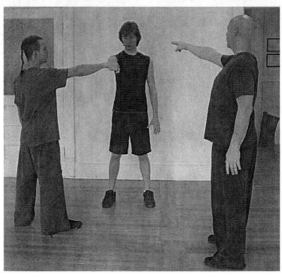

Section Two

Elucidation
of the Classic Texts

楊澄甫

太极拳十精華

Yang Cheng-Fu's

Ten Essentials of Tai Chi Chuan

Recorded by Chen Wei-Ming

Key # 1, Flex The Neck But Keep The Crown Of The Head Strong.

Keeping the crown strong means to maintain the neck upright and the face neutral, and to pay full attention to the crown of the head. Do not tense up, otherwise the neck gets rigid and Qi will be blocked. You must keep the spirit light and natural. If the neck is not neutrally loosened and the crown is not strong, it is impossible to uplift the spirit.

第一，虚领顶劲.

顶劲者，头容正直，神贯于顶也．不可用力，用力则项强，气血不能流通，须有虚灵自然之意．非有虚领顶劲，则精神不能提起也.

The crown of the head is lifted as though you were suspended from a string attached to the ceiling. Uplifting the spirit means that your awareness is heightened or that you are able to perceive everything around you while you simultaneously maintain focus on the opponent. The spine will more naturally lengthen if the crown of the head is lifted, therefore allowing the Qi to rise to the second dan-tien.

Key # 2, Concave The Chest Slightly And Keep The Back Long

Concaving the chest slightly means to curve the shoulders forward slightly but keep the chest hollow, and move Qi downward to the Dan Tian. The chest should not exert forward, otherwise the Qi will be static in the chest causing the top to be heavy and the heels to lift. When the back is long, Qi is attached to the back. If the chest is concaved slightly, the back will be long naturally and if the back is long, energy will spontaneously beam from the back to make one invincible.

第二，含胸拔背．

含胸着，胸略内含，使气沉于丹田也．　胸忌挺起，挺起则气拥胸际，上重下轻，脚根易于浮起．　拔背者，气贴于背也，能含胸则自能拔背，能拔背则能力由脊发，所向无敌也．

Sinking the chest, draping the shoulders and straightening the spine are all interrelated. You cannot overdo one of them without negatively affecting the others. You can drape the shoulders too much and curve the spine and cause the pectoral muscles in the chest to contract too much. You can also lift the thoracic spine too much and this will raise the shoulders and lift the chest. In other words, you just have to find your "happy place." You can test your structure with the Eight Stabilities test until you find the perfect frame (Chuan Jia).

*Remember to draw the energy up from the floor through the points in the bottom of the feet, through the legs and waist and then out through the hands. You should **not** be relying on muscular strength in the chest, shoulders or back during this testing (or anytime for that matter). When you find this happy place during the testing it should feel unusually easy to hold the frame. It should not feel as though you are fighting against the tester.*

Key # 3, Loosen The Waist

The waist is the commander in chief of the body. Only if the waist is flexible, the feet will be powerful and the lower body will be stable and solid. The free maneuverability of the waist is the foundation of the dynamics of Insubstantial and Substantial. This is the reason we often say, "the waist is the fountain of life," and "if one is not as powerful as one should be, one should look for the answer in the waist and legs."

第三，松腰.

腰为一身之主宰，能松腰然后两足有力，下盘稳固；虚实变化皆由腰转动，故曰："命意源头在腰隙"，"有不得力比于腰腿求之也."

Because the weight of the upper torso rests along the L4 and L5 vertebrae (more on one than the other depending on the amount of natural lordosis in your lumbar spine), one or both of these vertebrae can slide forward due to the oblique orientation of the sacrum. In Tai Chi we solve this dilema by nutation of the sacrum (tucking or scooping the tailbone forward). This decreases the lumbar lordosis and directs the weight of the upper torso into the legs where it can be utilized for power.

It is important to note here that there is generally a marked difference in the pelvic areas of men and women. The difference is the amount of natural lordosis (curvature) in the lumbar-sacral region of the spine. Women tend toward more natural lordosis than men. When men scoop the tailbone there is a natural lift in the lower abdominal area (the pelvic belly). Because in women the distance is longer from the tip of the tailbone to the pelvic belly you will have to remind most women to lift this area in addition to scooping the tailbone. Of course, there will be exceptions to this on both ends of the spectrum.

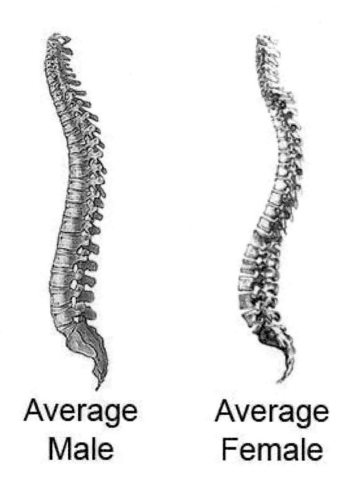

Average
Male

Average
Female

Loosening the waist is a perfect balance between nutation of the sacrum (scooping the tailbone) and bending at the hinge of the hips. In other words, you can bend at the hinge too much and counter-nutate the sacrum and create lordosis in the lumbar spine. You can scoop the tailbone too much and make it difficult to bend at the hinge of the hips. Moreover, being loose or "Song" is a result of a perfect balance between relaxing the muscles and creating structural integrity with the tendons and bones. The structural integrity of the hips and waist is created by both scooping the tailbone and opening the Gwa or, as Wu Yu-Qing says, "hollow the crotch and protect the hips." To open the Gwa or "hollow the crotch" involves a slight abduction of the thighs. You should notice that the gluteus medius muscles will activate to keep the sacrum from wobbling (protecting the hips). Of course you cannot move the thighs outwardly without a counter-balance to keep the movement in check. Move the ankle bones toward the center (adduct) very slightly to create the Yin of the thigh's Yang. This is how you create Peng Jing in the legs.

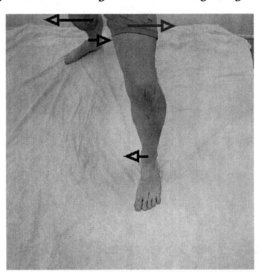

Key # 4, Differentiate Insubstantial and Substantial

Tai Chi Chuan regards differentiating Insubstantial and Substantial the most important philosophy of its teaching. If the whole body is sitting on the right leg, the right leg is Substantial and the left leg is

Insubstantial. Conversely, the left leg is Substantial and the right is Insubstantial. If Insubstantial and Substantial are differentiated, the turning and moving will be light and effortless. Otherwise, the gait will be heavy and lack vitality. It is also impossible to be balanced and therefore one can be easily manipulated about.

第四，分虚实.

太极拳术以分虚实为第一义，如全身皆坐在右腿，则右腿为实，左腿为虚；全身皆坐在左腿，则左腿为实，右腿为虚. 虚实能分，而后转动轻灵，毫不费劲；如不能分，则万步重滞，自立不稳，而易为人所牵动.

The ability to smoothly transition from Insubstantial to Substantial is a direct result of loosening the waist. The ability to release power into your opponent is a result of correctly maintaining Insubstantial and Substantial. Empty must always contain the element of full and full must always contain the element of empty. In other words, empty is never completely Insubstantial and Substantial is never completely full. Advance must contain retreat and vice-versa.

Key # 5, Sink The Shoulders And Drop The Elbows

When we say sinking the shoulders, it means to loosen up the shoulders and let them hang. If sinking the shoulders cannot be achieved, the shoulders would be lifted up, and consequently Qi would go upward and then the whole body would lose the ability to secure strength. When we say dropping the elbows, it means to drop the elbows downward with gravity naturally. If the elbows are suspended or uplifted, the shoulders can never be sunken as mentioned above. As a result, the thrust of the force cannot go far, and the weakening of the strength is almost equivalent of being slashed by an external force.

第五，沉肩坠肘．

沉肩者，肩松开下垂也． 若不能松垂，两肩端起，则气亦随之而上，全身皆不得力矣． 坠肘者，肘往下松坠之意，肘若悬起，则肩不能沉，放人不远，近于外家之断劲矣

As I said earlier, the sinking of the shoulders is directly related to the concaving of the chest. The elbows should sink or drop but the armpit area should not have a feeling of contraction. In other words, do not squeeze the armpits closed.

Do not sink the elbows too low nor raise them too high. The highest posture relative to the elbow is Crane Spreads Wings (Bai He Liang Chi). The elbow cannot reach up beyond the top of the shoulder. This is for three reasons. First, if it suddenly became necessary, the arm could not be drawn down quickly enough to protect the midsection. Second, the opponent can attack at your upper elbow *and push you backward. Third, the structure cannot hold enough*

force from above.

The lowest posture relative to the elbow is Punch Downward (groin

punch) in which the elbow cannot dip below the knee. This is true

for Needle at the Sea Bottom as well. Basically, the same reasons

apply here. First, you cannot raise up quickly enough. Second, your

opponent can take advantage by pushing you down. Third, the

structure will fail when force is applied.

Key # 6, Use The Conscious Mind Not The Force

Tai Chi Chuan discipline says, "The essence of Tai Chi Chuan is to use the conscious mind not the force." When practicing Tai Chi Chuan, one must keep the whole body loosened and do not make unwieldy effort to cause the inertia in tendons, bones, and blood, which is similar to putting shackles on oneself. Only if the whole body is loosened, is one able to segue from one pose to another as one desires. One may be in disbelief and may say, "if strength is not practiced, how can strength grow?" The answer is that the body has Jing and Luo like the earth has rivers and streams. Water runs smoothly if the rivers and streams are not blocked; by the same token, Qi flows freely when Jing and Luo are not closed. If the whole body is rigid, Qi and blood will stop flowing, turning and moving would be difficult, and as a result, the whole body will become unstable even if only one hair is pulled. However, if the conscious mind is utilized instead of the force, wherever the conscious mind goes, Qi arrives. Thus, Qi and blood will flow freely, day after day, circulating the whole body again and again ceaselessly. After practicing for a long time, one will gain the true inner strength, which is what Tai Chi Chuan discipline says, "The extreme solidity and strength are obtained from the extreme softness and flexibility." The arms of advanced Tai Chi Chuan practitioners are like iron covered with cotton – exceptionally heavy. Martial arts practitioners who have expertise in external skills often only know how to use external force. For them, when the force is not used, nothing else exists but shallowness and insignificance. Therefore, this kind of force is only a superficial strength with no depth. Utilizing the force instead of the conscious mind should not be encouraged because that's the easiest way to be eradicated.

第六，用意不用力.

太极拳论云："此全是用意不用力." 练太极拳全身松开，不能有分毫之拙劲，以留滞于筋骨血脉之间以自缚束，然后能轻灵变化，圆转自如. 或疑不用力何以能长力？ 盖人身之有经络，如地之有沟洫，沟洫不塞而水行，经络不闭则气通. 如浑身僵劲满经络，气血停滞，转动不灵，牵一发而全身动矣. 若不用力而用意，意之所至，气即至焉，如是气血流注，日日贯输，周流全身，无时停滞. 久久练习，则得真正内劲，即太极拳论中所云："极柔软然后极坚钢" 也. 太

极拳功夫熟练之人，臂膊如锦里铁，分量极沉；练外家拳者，用力则
显有力，不用力时，则甚轻浮，可见其力乃外劲浮面之劲也。　不用
意而用力，最易引动，不足尚也．

The concept of using the conscious mind instead of force can be likened to a river. The banks of a river direct the water where it should go. Qi, like water, needs to be directed in this manner. This is done by proper alignment in the frame. A river without banks is not a river at all, but a swamp. The water is purposeless and stagnant. So is the Qi stagnant when the body is too soft and relaxed. Conversely, when a river is dammed, no water flows at all. The Qi is similarly dammed by excessive muscular strength. When the structural integrity of the frame is being maintained by the conscious mind, we say that the body has achieved the state of Song (pronounced "sown"). Song is the term that is typically translated as "relaxed" but obviously this is not a Western concept. Relaxed in the West has something to do with a Lazyboy recliner and a remote control. In the East, Song means that every part of the body is loosened and lengthened and held in place by minute actions initiated by the mind and energized by the Qi.

Key # 7, The Lower Body Should Follow The Upper Body Or Visa Versa—Other Parts Of The Body Should Follow Whichever Part Is The Lead.

The seventh key means, in Tai Chi Chuan discipline, "even though the feet are the roots, the strength is initiated from the legs. Similarly, the waist is the commander in chief, but oftentimes the fingers are the executors of the action. From the feet to the legs to the waist, everything should coordinate as a whole to execute any action." Hands, waist, feet, and eyes should move harmoniously together—that is why we say that different parts of the body should follow one another coordinately. If, during an execution of an action, one part of the body stops moving, it will throw the entire practice into disarray.

第七，上下相随．
上下相随者，即太极拳论中所云："其跟在脚，发于腿，主宰于腰，形于手指，由脚而腿而腰，总须完整一气"也．手动，腰动，足动，眼神亦随之动，如是方可谓之上下相随，有一不动，即散乱也．

The upper and lower parts of the body being in coordination is speaking of the three external harmonies: hands and feet in harmony, elbows and knees in harmony and shoulders and waist in harmony. This is, of course, concerning postures in motion and not so much how the posture looks when you are standing still. This is discussed at length in the section on the Six Harmonies, Eight Gates and Five Steps.

Key # 8, Synchronize The Internal With The External

The focus of Tai Chi Chuan practice is the spirit. It says that "the Spirit is the master and the body is its slave." If the spirit is high, the movements of the body are light and effortless. The poses are nothing but the opening and closing of Insubstantial and Substantial. The opening means not only the opening of the hands and feet but also the heart and the conscious mind. Likewise, the closing means not only the physical closing of the hands and feet but also the heart and the conscious mind at the same time. If the internal and external can be harmonized, the integration of the entire body would be seamless.

第八，内外相合．
太极拳所练在神，故云："神为主帅，身为驱使．" 精神能提得起，自然举动轻灵． 架子不外虚实开合． 所谓开着，不但手足开，心意亦舆之俱开． 所谓和者，不但手足合，心意亦之俱合． 能内外合为一气，则浑然无间矣．

Synchronizing the Internal with the External is speaking of the relationship of the Three Internal Harmonies (San Nei He) with the Three External Harmonies (San Wai He). When the Internal and the External are working in unity then the Spirit (awareness) is hightened. You are able to sense your opponents actions before they manifest and your own thoughts are instantaneously action because your conscious mind already resides in every part of your body poised to act on your every whim.

Key # 9, Be Continuous Without Interruption

The external force generated by martial artists who only practice external skills is unwieldy. Their movement has a beginning and an ending - sometimes it lasts for a long time and sometimes it stops. When the previous force is exhausted and the succeeding force has not been produced, this is the best opportunity for others to initiate an attack. Tai Chi Chuan manipulates the conscious mind, not the physical force. From the beginning to the end, it repeats the cycle over and over again perpetually without interruption. It is often said that "it is like the never-ending flow of the Yangtze River," and it is also said, "the movement of the force of Tai Chi Chuan is like the endless extraction of the silk thread from the cocoon." The essence of the sayings is that all the movements in Tai Chi Chuan should flow together seamlessly with one Qi.

第九，相连不断.

外家拳术，其劲乃后天拙劲，故有起有止，有续有断，旧力已尽，新力未生，此时最易为人所乘. 太极拳用意不用力，自始直终，绵绵不断，周而复始，循环无穷. 原所谓 "如长江大河，涛涛不决，" 又曰 "运劲如抽丝"，皆言其贯串一气也.

Being continuous without interruption is speaking of both the internal and external aspects of this concept. When practicing the 108 movement form the optimal time from beginning to end is 20 minutes. There is a 2 minute window on either end of the spectrum to make allownaces for taller or shorter persons ... taller persons finishing between 20 and 22 minutes because of the length of their frames and shorter persons finishing between 18 and 20 minutes. Any longer than this and the form will become "stopped"; meaning that the continuity has been broken. In other words, if it takes you longer than 20 minutes to do the form then you are stopping and starting each posture instead of smoothly transitioning and continuing the flow. This is the external aspect of this key. Internally speaking, if you allow the Jing to waver between postures then this is an opportunity for an opponent to take advantage. The hands are the most obvious place to observe the continuity of the Jing. If the energy in the fingers pulsates; meaning that in Brush Knee, for instance, you extend and energize the fingers but if you allow that extention to waver during transitioning then the Jing has left the fingers. Where the mind goes the energy follows. If you see the Jing leave your opponents hand you have seen his mind leave his hand. This is the opportunity to attack his hand. If the Jing is not in a particular body part then "Ting Jing" or Listening Skill is hindered in that part. Withdrawing the Jing is leaving. I often have heard my Sifu say "don't leave before I am coming". If the Jing leaves the hand it stands to reason that the Jing is leaving other less obvious parts as well. You must search yourself.

Key # 10, Find Calmness in the Movements

In martial arts that only address external skills, the ability to jump and walk is highly encouraged and the practitioners exhaust their strength and deplete the Qi. Therefore, after practicing, no one can be without panting. Tai Chi Chuan manipulates movements through calmness. Even though one is physically moving, calmness resides within. Hence, the slower the movement, the better the result. Breath should be long and deep, Qi sinks downward to the Dan Tian, and consequently blood vessel expansion can be prevented. Practitioners should ponder upon this to get the true meaning of Tai Chi Chuan.

第十，动中求静.
外家拳术，以跳 躧 为能，用尽气力，故练习之后，无不喘气者. 太极拳以静御动，虽动尤静，故 练架子愈慢愈好. 慢则呼吸深长，气沉丹田，自无血脉偾张之弊．　学者细心休 会，庶可得其意焉．

Finding calmness or stillness in the movements can only be achieved when the body is not exerted too forcefully and the breath is kept deep and even. I often tell my students about a very important breathing (Qi Gong) exercise called "In-Out In-Out Don't Stop". This is to remind them NOT to hold their breath between postures. Holding the breath will lead to panting because it inhibits oxygen from reaching the muscles as they are doing the work which, of course, is exactly when they need it. Keeping the breath long and even while practicing the form will lead to aerobic enhancement which leads to better health and the ability to continue fighting for longer periods of time if neccessary. Do not misinterpret this key to mean that you are not performing hard work while practicing Tai Chi, quite the contrary, it has often been said that performing the 108 movement form is the equivelant of "horse sitting" for 20 minutes. Also keep in mind that most reputable aged masters of Tai Chi advocate practicing the form six to eight times without a break... this is over two hours of continual movement. Fu Zhong-Wen said "only [practicing] in this way can a student catch the feeling of real kung fu and be able to develop martial skills."

武汝清

太极拳论

The Treatise of Wu Yu-Qing

The Treatise of Wu Yu-Qing

Tai Chi Chuan is all about Yin-Yang and Insubstantial-Substantial. Only if you grasp the meaning of Yin-Yang then you are able to understand advance and retreat. Certainly advance is to go forward, but you should keep retreat in mind while advancing. Similarly, retreat is to withdraw, but there might be an opportunity to advance while retreating. The pivotal point here is to loosen the neck, strengthen the crown of the head, elongate the back, and concave the chest slightly. By doing so, the spirit will be uplifted automatically. Sinking Qi to dan-tien, hollowing the crotch and protecting the hips, you are able to move around freely and with agility. Elbows better stay bent, because when keeping them bent they reserve the ability to extend, and as a result, you may gain advantage by pushing forward. Knees should be bent, because bending position gives you the capability to thrust and by doing so it makes the thrust powerful. When sparring with opponents, you should make hands contact first and then focus on finding out the opponent's strength level. Refrain yourself and let the opponent lead. Get to know the opponent but do not reveal yourself to him. Once you gather sufficient information about the opponent, you are able to retreat no matter which direction the opponent advances. Consequently, your opponent is going against the flow and you are going with it. The secret here is to loosen your shoulders, let your waist take control, ground your feet, and all the body parts take orders from your mind. Every move moves every part of the body, and once it is still every part of the body is still. From top to bottom, when the entire body is united by Qi, it stands like a balance, moves like a wheel, and strikes back from all directions. At this point, you become invincible. Strike your opponent before his action is fully initiated—we call it "striking the budding thrust." Wait in calmness and then strike your opponent's incoming attack before it is full executed—we call it "striking the incoming attack." Strike your opponent after his first attempt fails and tries to gather energy for the second come back—we call it "striking the second wind." Through practice and study, by observation and contemplation, you are able to master Tai Chi Chuan and eventually to reach a state of enlightenment.

武汝清

太极拳论

夫拳名太极者，阴阳虚实也．阴阳明然后知进退，进固是进，进中有退，步退仍 是进，退中隐有进机．此中转关，在于虚领顶劲，而拔背含胸，则精神提得起；气沉丹田而里裆护臀，则周旋便捷．肘宜曲，曲而能伸，则支撑得势．膝宜蓄，蓄而能发，则发劲有力．至与人交手，手先着力，只听人劲，务要由人，不要有己；务要知人，不要使人知己．知人则上下前后左右自能引进落空，则人背我顺．此中转关在乎松肩，主宰于腰，立根在脚，但听命于心．一动无有不动，一静无有不静．上下一气，即所谓立如秤准，活似车轮，支撑八面，所向无敌．　人劲将来，未能发出，我即打去，谓之 "打闷劲"．　人劲已来，我早静待，着身即便打去，所 谓 "打来劲"．人劲已落空，将欲换劲，我随打去，此谓 "打回劲"．　由此体验，留心揣摩，自能从心所欲，阶及神明焉．

I have included the Treatise of Wu Yu Qing because I know that it is important to corroborate anything that you believe to be true with at least two sources. Without at least two reputable sources you could take one misunderstood idea and be miles of course in no time at all. It is imperative to stay balanced...even in our philosophy. All of his concepts concerning when to strike the opponent will be discussed in volume two 'Anatomy of Tai Chi Pushing Hands.'

48   Section Three

Section Three

Achieving Conscious Movement

Great-Grandmaster Dr. Hu Yuen-Chou at 83

From the Ground Up

"Sound fighting is rooted in the feet, grows in the legs, is mastered by the waist and functions through the fingers."

I am sure that you all know this most important proverb of Chinese martial arts (and if you didn't, then you do now). This proverb is speaking of the way the power travels through the body and into an opponent. In teaching structural alignment, however, I do not begin with the feet except for general placement. I begin with the legs and waist. As you will recall, Yang Cheng-Fu said, "if one is not as powerful as one should be, one should look for the answer in the waist and legs." The largest muscle groups in your body are in the waist and legs. These two muscle groups control the majority of the body movements which comprise each Tai Chi posture.

In teaching the structure of the legs and waist I always begin with the most basic concepts and as the student progresses I introduce more and more detail, always building on the first concept I taught. As Yang Ban-Hou said, "first we learn the feet and inches and then the hundredth parts and the thousandth parts." So I will begin this chapter in the same manner.

Look first at the bow stance (Gong Bu) which is used for the majority of the Tai Chi postures. The feet should be placed hip-width distance apart (I measure this from the front of the hip bones straight down to the inside of the feet) and then approximately three times that distance (measured diagonally from heel to heel) from front to back. The front foot should point directly forward and the rear foot should be placed anywhere from 60° to 45° from directly forward. 45° is optimal, but this range is dependant upon the flexibility of the Achilles tendon (see the section on exercises to improve your Tai Chi). Beyond 60° is not acceptable because it prevents the inward rotation of the rear thigh and is contraindicated because it allows the weakest part of the knee joint to hold the stress of the body weight.

Since I do teach movement from one posture to another quite early (in comparison to the traditional five years of standing postures before learning the moving form), it is important to note that in practicing the moving bow stance the distance between the feet from front to back may be a little shorter than specified depending on the flexibility and strength of the student. The primary alignment adjustment following the placement of the feet will be on the front thigh (full). First, imagine that you can lift the skin on the inside of your thigh near the knee. You will lift this area toward the ceiling (or sky) then draw the area on the outside of the thigh near the crease at the hip down toward the ground. The center of the kneecap should now be aligned between the 2nd and 3rd toes of the front foot.

The next structural adjustment will be on the rear (or empty) thigh. You will move the skin on the outside of the upper area of the rear thigh toward the front. The skin on the inside of the rear thigh moves to the rear. In essence, the rear (empty) thigh is rotating inwardly.

As you begin to understand these concepts I will move along to the next level of this teaching. Return your attention to the front thigh and think about the earlier concept of lifting up at the inside of the knee and sinking down at the outside of the hip ... essentially you are rotating the thigh to the outside so I will call this an outer spiral on the front thigh.

Now you have an outer spiraling energy on the front thigh and an inwardly spiraling energy on the rear thigh. These two opposing forces that are spiraling in opposite directions create structural strength in the hips and waist. I call this concept the "dish rag effect" because it resembles the action of wringing water from a rag. As you know, the more you twist the rag on each end the center of the rag becomes stiff and strong like a rope. This structural integrity you have just created in the hips and waist needs to be created in the knees as well. In order to accomplish this, you will use the "dish rag effect" on the shins. You will apply an inward spiral on the front shin and, of course, an outward spiral on the rear shin. Keep in mind that you are not wrenching these joints with all of your might. Remember you are using the mind and not force.

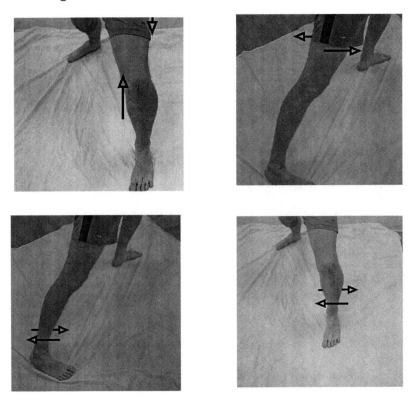

This creates safe, strong, healthy knees that are full of energy. Consequently, legs that are full of energy (Jing) respond quickly to your thoughts because your mind is now residing in your legs.

The next adjustment is performed in two areas. Move your ankle bones slightly inward and abduct (separate) your thighs slightly. This is called keeping the Gwa (groin) open. Again, let me reiterate that none of these adjustments are overly forceful and some may be no more than a thought for you or a tiny twinge of energy in that particular direction. The only way to know what is "just right" for you is to test the Jing with the Eight Stabilities test.

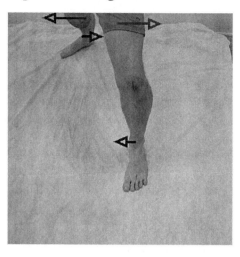

Keeping the Gwa open is as much about maintaining softness and pliabililty in the waist as it is creating strength and stability in the lower back by activating the gluteus medius muscles to keep the sacrum from shifting. Remember Wu Yu Qing said "hollow the crotch and protect the hips." Maintaining the spiraling energy on the shins while moving the ankles inward and the thighs outward will create a feeling as though your feet were glued to the floor and create Peng energy in the legs. Although I do not advocate barefoot Tai Chi in general, I do suggest discarding your shoes and socks while you are beginning to learn these concepts. It is much easier to feel how the weight and energy are equally distributed in the bottoms of the feet if you are barefoot. You should be aware if the weight feels as though it were more along the outside edge of one foot or the inside edge of the other or more in the toes or heels. If the weight feels as though it is not equally distributed in the feet then the correction would be in the waist and legs.

The weight distribution in the Tai Chi bow stance is 70% in the front leg and 30% in the rear leg. The energy distribution is 50% in each, meaning that the legs are exerting the same force into the ground with each foot - not only to the front and rear but also to the left and right. The weight distribution tells us which way the thighs and shins are spiraling. In the Substantial or 70% leg (in this case the front) the thigh is spiraling outwardly and the shin is spiraling inwardly. As with all things relating to energy in Tai Chi, there must be an equal balance on both sides - too much on one side means not enough on the other . As I am very fond of telling my younger students , "Tai Chi operates on the Goldie Locks and the Three Bears principle." Everything in Tai Chi must be "just right." That being said, the Instubstantial or rear leg (the 30% leg here), as you will recall, has an inward spiral on its thigh and an outward spiral on its shin to keep the Peng Jing in the knee and to keep the weight distribution in the rear foot equanimous.

This is how we create perfect roundness and perfect squareness (Peng Jing). This means that you do not have too much roundness nor too much squareness in the legs (and similarly in the arms). An excess of roundness creates weakness and an insufficiency of roundness is weak. It is the same with squareness.

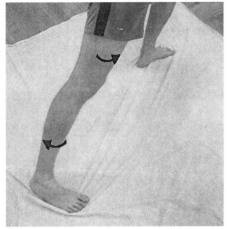

Teacher's Note:

We must keep it simple for beginners. New beginners would be completely overwhelmed by these concepts. "First we learn the feet and inches, and then the hundredth parts and thousandth parts." So introduce these concepts slowly! With new beginners I am normally only concerned that they understand and implement the placement of the feet. After approximately 2 weeks to a month I will then add the inner and outer rotations of the thighs. As I see the student gaining understanding I will add the spiraling of the shins.

Sinking the hips or bending at the hinge where the legs connect to the upper torso is the next step on our way to achieving conscious movement. I have found that it is sometimes difficult for new beginners to comprehend this concept because they have never really bent over at their hinge but merely rounded their backs to reach for something on the ground. I have devised a methodology for helping these people to find their hinges.

Squat all the way to your heels. Come half-way up and place your index finger on the place where your body is folded in half (at your hips). This is your hinge. Any bending of the body will happen there - not in your back.

Finding a balance or "happy place" between bending at the hinge and scooping the tailbone forward is what we call "sinking the hips." Of course here we find yet another place to remind students of the "Goldie Locks and Three Bears" principle. Not too much scoop on the tailbone and not too much folding at the hinge. Over-nutation of the sacrum (scooping the tailbone too forcefully) will cause the hips to be stiff and brings an inordinate amount of weight into the area above the kneecap of the front knee. Conversely sinking into the hinge too much will cause counter-nutation of the sacrum and thus make the hips and waist too limp and causes too much weight to move into the front of the forward knee just below the kneecap. This also displaces the energy in the bottom of the front foot moving it into the toes especially when transitioning between postures. It should be obvious by now that one small error in the frame causes a domino effect thoughout the body.

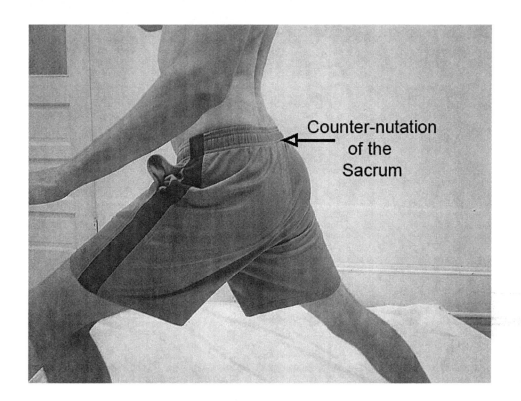

Counter-nutation of the Sacrum

Now that I have divulged these concepts for the *Gong Bu* (bow stance) I will give you the advice Musashi gave "from one thing know a thousand things." You will take these concepts and apply them to the other stances.

Ding Bu is the "T" stance or Repulse Monkey stance. This stance is approximately half the length of the Gong Bu. The weight distribution of Insubstantial and Substantial is reversed in Ding Bu. This reversal of Insubstantial and Substantial causes a reversal of all of the spiraling energies in the legs but not the energies which create the opening of the Gwa. The opening of the Gwa is a constant throughout all of the

Tai Chi postures.

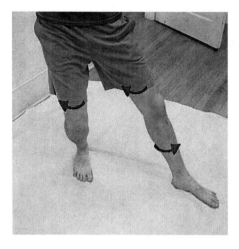 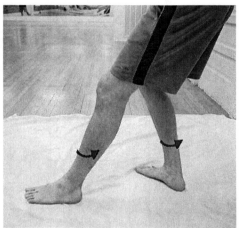

Xu Bu or Empty Stance takes two forms in Tai Chi; heel lifted and toe lifted. You utilize the heel lifted version in the postures White Stork Spreads Wings, High Pat on Horse, Needle at the Sea Bottom and Sit Back and Ride the Tiger. The toe lifted Xu Bu is utilized in the postures Play the Pipa, Raise Hands and Step Forward and Fist Under Elbow. Since the Substantial and Insubstantial qualities of these Xu Bu stances is the same as the Ding Bu all of the same rules apply to the legs and waist. Remember, as well, that Insubstantial is never completely empty. You must maintain energy in the feet. For the heel up Xu Bu you should press the ball of the front foot into the floor and for the toes up Xu Bu you should press the heel of the front foot into the floor.

Pu Bu is the Snake Creeps Down stance. The length of this stance is the same as the Gong Bu although it may appear slightly longer because the rear foot pivots on the heel from its position at 45° to 135° from the front foot. The width of the feet is still hip width. It is a very common error to narrow the width between the feet in this stance. As you will remember the outer spiral on the thigh follows Substantiality meaning that even though you would like to rotate your rear thigh inwardly in this stance this is a big no no. The rear knee has a propensity toward drooping in. This is contraindicated for obvious reasons concerning the health of your knees.

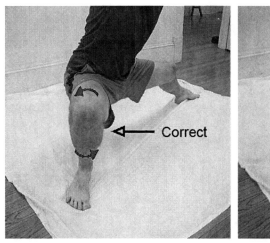
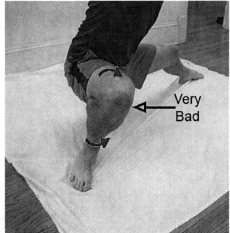

Du Li Bu or one-legged stance is utilized for Golden Rooster Stands on One Leg and all of the kicking postures. All of the one-legged postures have an inward spiral on the standing thigh and an outer spiral on the standing shin. Spread the toes creating a wider foundation to enhance balance ... do not grip the floor with the toes. There are three types of kicks in the 108 movement form. Separation of Toe left and right uses an upward motion for striking (separating the toes on the standing foot from those on the kicking foot) so we say this is Kicking Upward. Kicking Downward is used for Striking with the Sole because the knee of the kicking leg is lifted higher than the target and therefore the foot travels at a slight downward angle to the target. Lotus kick uses centrifugal force to strike its target. Kicking should always be tall. Do not move your head closer to the knee as you kick as this is a common error. Follow Yang Cheng-Fu's first Key and keep the crown of the head lifted.

The *Wu Chi* stance which appears at the commencement, conclusion and Cross Hands is an anomaly in the Tai Chi form. Similar to the square horse of many other martial arts it utilizes an inner rotation of **both** thighs and an outer rotation on **both** shins.

The Mystery Stance ... Bend the Bow to Shoot the Tiger is done in a special Gong Bu in which the feet are on the same line and not the hip width or three line stance utilized for all other bow stance postures. The toes of the Substantial (front) foot are turned inwardly about 10° to 30°. This stance more closely resembles the Choy Li Fut *Ding Ji Ma* or the Hung Gar *Gong Bu Ma*. The reason for this variance is structural integrity. You are delivering a strike along a perpindicular line from your leg structure. If you utilize a regular Tai Chi bow stance the reaction force from your strike will unbalance you. Test this concept with the Eight Stabilities test.

Bend the Bow to Shoot the Tiger

Drawing Up from the Earth

Drawing Up from the Earth

Now here is one more level of intricacy that will get you one step closer to perfect Tai Chi. There is a pressure point on the bottom of your foot just in front of your heel (*Zu An*). In the Bow Stance (Gong Bu) initiate a small lift up from the floor at that point as though there was a tack under your foot that you do not want to step on (you really have to practice this). You must maintatin contact with the floor on all parts of the foot as before (except for the Zu An point which is less than a square centimeter). You will find that when you master lifting this point away from the floor that the outer rotation of the thigh and the inner rotation of the shin seems to happen naturally. You will perform a similar action on the Insubstantial leg as well but with a different acupunture point. The *Yong Chuan* point just behind the ball of the foot in line with the space between the second and third toes. This is what the ancient masters meant when they spoke of gathering energy from the earth while practicing Tai Chi.

Now, you will take this action and move with it. The Zu An point follows the Substantial leg and the Yong Chuan point follows the Insubstantial leg. When transitioning between postures or when you are in a Repulsed Monkey (Ding Bu) or Snake Creeps Down (Pu Bu) stance you will reverse the emphasis and those two points on your feet. When you initiate the emptying of the front leg you will move the emphasis from the Zu An point of the front foot to the Yong Chuan point of the front foot and do the same in reverse for the back foot.

This action of drawing up energy from the earth will energize your entire frame. You will also notice an unusual sensitivity and rootedness while practicing pushing hands.

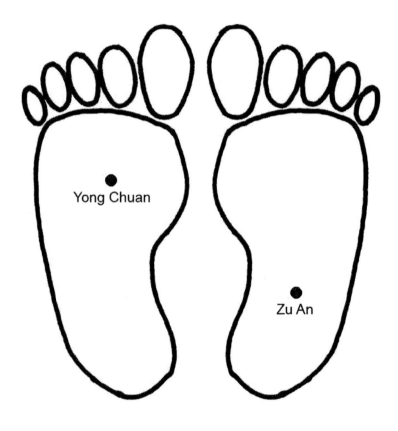

Straight But Not Straight

When you straighten the legs (empty the legs), either moving the weight from the back leg to the front leg or vice versa, it is not uncommon for beginner students to take the Insubstantial leg to full extension or to the locked out position. This is a no-no. Try this experiment. Take a Repulsed Monkey (Ding Bu) stance and bring your front leg into full extension (locked out). Try to push energy into your front foot. Now move your front leg just out of full extension and see how much more energy you are able to move into the front foot. Now combine that with the inner spiral on the front thigh and balance it out with the outer spiral on the front shin. Now your whole foot should be in contact with the floor like a suction cup. This increase in power is especially noticeable while performing *Lu* (roll-back). I had you experiment with the front leg first because it is easier for your mind to grasp new concepts when they are right in front of you.

Now you can try a similar experiment on the rear leg.

Take a bow stance (Gong Bu) and fully extend your rear leg (lock it out). Although you should be able to more easily square your hips in this stance, the weight distribution on the back foot will not be equanimous. More weight will be on the inside edge of the foot starting from the big toe and ending on the inside edge of the heel. In order to equalize distribution of weight in foot you must unlock (soften) the rear knee with an outer spiral on the rear shin until the weight is equally distributed throughout the bottom of the rear foot.

So it is generally said that the Insubstantial leg is "straight but not straight, bent but not bent" meaning that it is extended as much as possible without locking it. Locking the Instubstantial leg also eliminates the possiblity of using Spring Jing (Tan Jing 彈精) because you will have to stop , unlock the knee and then continue moving.

Straight but not straight applies to the arms and fingers as well. In extending the elbows you should not take them to the "locked-out" position. By maintaining a slight bent in the elbows you are keeping some potential energy stored up and ready to explode (Fa Jing) into the opponent when the oppotunity presents itself. In extending the fingers they should also remain slightly bent.

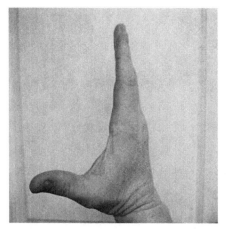 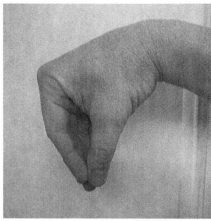

Teacher's Notes:

In teaching Tai Chi concepts to new beginner students I begin the first class with a discussion of the five "stay downs". These cues are easy to comprehend and I do not overwhelm the students with too much information (TMI).

The Five "Stay Downs" (New beginners)

1. The shoulders stay down
2. The chest stays down
3. The elbows stay down
4. The butt stays down (scoop the tailbone)
5. The back heel stays down

After the students can implement the five "stay downs" correctly I beging to introduce the concept of the five "sinks."

The Five "Sinks" (2 months or more)

1. Sink the shoulders
2. Sink the chest
3. Sink the elbows
4. Sink the wrists
5. Sink the waist

大人⋯

大拳架

Big Man ... Big Frame

Big Man ... Big Frame

There has been much debate in recent years about which Frame is best. Yang Cheng-Fu did the Large Frame. Yang Shao-Hou did the Small Frame. Yang Jian-Hou did the Medium Frame. Some people have speculated that the Frame became larger over time because it was refined by the second and third generations and therefore, Large Frame is best. Some people speculate that since Yang Shao-Hou was reknowned for his fighting abilities that Small Frame must be better for fighting and Large Frame must be used only for health oriented Tai Chi practice. While these arguments seem to be based on reasonable thought the truth is found in simple physics.

Yang Cheng-Fu did his Tai Chi bigger because he had no other logical choice ... he was a big man. Yang Shao-Hou was smaller so his Tai Chi Frame was smaller. Any construction contractor will tell you that the structure of a larger, heavier building must be different than that of a smaller, lighter edifice. If your shoulders and hips are wider obviously your foundational stance will have to be wider. You can test this with the Eight Stabilities test.

There is another debate which has arisen in recent years concerning whether you should lean forward in the Gong Bu postures. This stems from photos of Yang Cheng-Fu that Tai Chi practitioners have been viewing since around 1934. Yang Cheng-Fu leaned forward because of a phenomenon that we are all too familiar with here in the West... the "beer belly". It is paramount to note here that Yang Cheng-Fu was obviously incredibly self-aware to know that he needed to lean forward in order to compensate for the additional mass in his lower abdominal area. He never taught students who were young and fit to lean forward.

Here in the West I often have students come to my classes with the classic "beer belly" and I do instruct these men to incline slightly forward (1/2" to 2" off dead plumb depending on the size of the belly). This is very slight and I always start with 1/2" and test the structure with the Eight Stabilities test until it is perfect. This is something I have to correct again and again until their bodies remember. If during the course of practicing Tai Chi these students become more fit and healthy I will have to correct their Frames bringing them back to a more plumb alignment as they lose weight.

Here you see a photo of Yang Cheng-Fu in Brush Knee posture with a slight forward incline.

Here you see a photo of Dr. Hu Yuen-Chou (a Closed-Door student of Yang Cheng-Fu) in Brush Knee posture with a plumb structural alignment. Notice that Dr. Hu is very fit even at 93 years of age.

Stand Like A Balance;
Turn Like A Wheel

This concept is really the upper torso's contribution to the structural integrity of your Tai Chi postures. Stand like a balance (or scale) means not leaning in any direction.

It is as though a steel rod were inserted into the crown of your head down along the inside of the spine and then exiting through the perineum and into the floor. In other words, a vertical plumb line runs through the body. The second most common error in Tai Chi practice is "butting" or leaning forward (the first is, of course, double-weightedness)

"Turn like a wheel" can only be accomplished after you can "stand like a balance." "Turning like a wheel" means that the upper torso rotates like a freewheel on the axis we created with that imaginary steel rod. This free turning on the plumb axis is how the waist directs the energy coming from the feet and legs out through the hands. There can be no resistance to this turning movement or the striking power will be decreased. Range of motion is another important factor for "turning like a wheel." Some students may lack the flexibility to turn their torsos enough to complete the posture.

Teacher's Notes:

This may be difficult for some people to grasp (not in their mind but in their body) because of neuro-muscular amnesia. For example, if a person is overweight and has been leaning slightly to the rear to compensate for the additional mass then his mind can forget what plumb is. When you move him into plumb, he will believe that he is leaning forward. Neuro-muscular amnesia could also stem from an injury the student has had which causes him to incline slightly in one direction or another. You must be especially patient with these persons because their bodies have truly forgotten what straight up and down feels like.

Stillness in Motion

Now that you have experienced these concepts in standing postures you can begin to delve into the next level of Tai Chi, which is moving from one posture to another. This is where Tai Chi can really get difficult.

Not only do you have to remember all of these inner and outer rotations and the sinks and stay downs, but you also have to move. Movement in Tai Chi is all about empty and full, transferring weight from one leg to the other and maintaining structural integrity while stepping forward, backward and sideways.

The inner and outer rotation of the thighs moves energy like a bullet spiraling out of a gun. As mentioned before, the Jing of each and every posture in the Tai Chi form has to be maintained throughout the body by the conscious mind. There can be no wavering of the intensity of the Jing. Each time you move from one posture to another you transfer weight from the full leg to the empty leg and in doing this the rotation of the thighs and shins reverses. This happens **during** the transfer, by the way, not at the beginning or the end.

Therefore, power is emitted by creating an Insubstantial leg from a Substsantial one. Of course, the Jing you are moving into the now

Substantial leg will be released when the weight is transferred again. This is a continuous process which begins at the commenecent of the form and ends only at the conclusion of the form. As mentioned before there can be no stopping and starting during the execution of the form and there can be no pulsating of the Jing. You may think that you would like to practice Fa Jing (explosive energy) in the 108 movement form but this is not the traditional method. Fa Jing is traditionally trained by executing single postures repeatedly. Shifting from Insubstantial to Substantial. The Yang family also used a spear to practice Fa Jing; thrusting it out again and again until the Jing reached the tip of the spear.

Of course there is the Small Circle set and the Fast Set for practicing Fa Jing after you have mastered emitting it by practicing the single posture method.

Teacher's notes:

The common error when students are first learning to walk (transition from one posture to another) is what I refer to as "rolling the weight". This occurs when students do not plant their toes before transitioning from Insubstantial to Substantial. "Rolling" then leads to "butting" and "butting" leads to really bad Tai Chi.

For teaching older persons (I will let you decide what constitutes an older person), I have found that requiring that they move at a certain or specific speed can lead to confusion. I usually do not require that they move too slowly until after they have memorized the shape of the posture. For example, I will place the student in front of a mirror and instruct him to shift the weight from the rear leg to the front leg while performing Partition of the Wild Horse's Mane and then shifting the weight to the rear leg and returning the hands to the "closed" position. This is repeated again and again at a medium speed. I tell the student to think of the shape of the posture only (how it looks at each end). I cue him to move his arms as though they were sliding in grooves in the air. This concept I cannot take full credit for. In his book *Karate-Do, My Way of Life*, Gichin Funakoshi explains that he practiced his katas (forms) so much that he wore out a place in the air for them. I use this method to teach many of the basic postures. After the student has memorized the shape of the posture I will instruct him in the Tai Chi walking method.

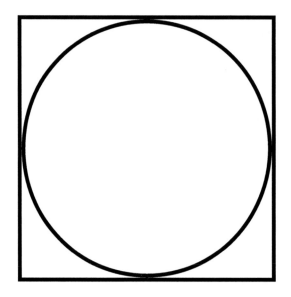

Perfect Roundness and Perfect Squareness

Perfect Roundness and Perfect Squareness

I have discussed roundness and squareness as they relate to the legs and now I will discuss how to they relate to the upper torso. I am speaking of creating Peng energy in the postures in the Tai Chi form that begin with the arms circling outward and then scooping under and together. The postures are Cross Hands, Separeation of Right and Left Toe, Strike with the Sole and, to a certain degree, the Turning Lotus Kick after Plain Cross Hands. I include this last posture because the same rules for the distance between the hands apply. Of course, roundness and suareness are applied to all of the Tai Chi postures. I begin with these particular postures because they are the biggest. There is a proverb in Chinese martial arts that says "little comes from big". So it is easier to learn roundness and suareness in the postures where the arms are extended more and then apply these concepts to smaller postures (where the elbows are closer to the body).

I always tell my students that the distance is about one meter, but that a Jing test (Eight Stabilities) is required to gauge the exact distance for their particular frame. The placement of the hands is another example of the "Goldie Locks and the Three Bears principle." The hands cannot be too close together, too far apart, too high nor too low. All of these would cause a weakness in the Frame.

The concept is that when force is applied to pull the hands apart you are able to hold them in and when force is applied to push the hands closer together you would be able to keep them apart. When force is applied upward or downward you are able to maintatin not only your position but your balance as well. All of this is without having to exert an inordinate amount of physical strength.

Cultivating the Breath

In Tai Chi practice there are two types of breathing. One that you cultivate for life and one that you cultivate for fighting.

When practicing the 108 movement form you are concerned with maintaining a long, even inhalation and an equally long and even exhalation. Holding one breath in or out is not permitted. The inhalation and exhalation are not specifically coordinated with closing and opening or gathering and emitting of Jing within any postures. When Li I-Yu discussed coordination of the breath with the postures in his "Five Character Secret" he is specifically discussing emitting Jing in pushing hands or fighting.

The second kind of Tai Chi breathing, according to Li I-Yu is coordinating the breath with the postures for the purpose of gathering and emitting Jing. The inhalation is coordinated with the gathering of Jing. Typically, this happens in the spaces between the postures. However, there are postures which are performed with an inhalation. Roll Back is considered a gathering posture and therefore is executed on an inhalation. Press is therefore executed on an exhalation. You should first practice this method with the single posture method of developing Fa Jing and you should practice every posture this way. You should also practice coordinating the breath with the thrust of the spear in the spear method of Fa Jing training.

Although you do not practice the 108 movement form in this way the breath is coordinated with the transitioning in the postures in the Fast set.

Teachers Notes:

I often tell my students to remember the most important breathing exercise: "in-out-in-out don't stop." Of course, the most difficult thing for beginners is continuing to breathe while concentrating intensely on other parts of their bodies.

The Seven Stars

Step Up to Seven Stars. You are probably familiar with this posture. But what are the seven stars? Is it is constellation? No. The Seven Stars are the head, the shoulders, the hands, the waist, the knees, the elbows and the feet. Step Up to Seven Stars is actually a poor translation of the original Chinese. This should be translated as "The Seven Stars Come Forward." According to Great Grandmaster Dr. Hu Yuen-Chou, this is a block up with the left arm and a punch underneath with the right hand. Of course, there is a hidden kick as well. You will notice that all of these Stars do move forward during the execution of this posture.

With a little time spent studying the Tai Chi Classics you will find many translations like this which have been misunderstood for many years. I advocate studying as many different translations of the texts as you can find. There may be some small point in a particular translation which speaks to you specifically as everyone has a different way of learning based on their life experiences. The reference section at the end of this text is also my recommended reading list.

Usage: The Soul of Tai Chi

You may be asking yourself, "Hey, this is a lot to think about....Why is all this necessary?" The answer lies at the heart of Tai Chi itself. Fighting. You may say "I do not believe in fighting." This is perfectly fine ... do not fight ... but the only way to get the maximum health benefits from the practice of Tai Chi is to practice in this manner. I read an interview a number of years ago with a prominent Chinese Tai Chi personality in which he stated that you could practice Tai Chi just for health without attention to these details and that you could not injure yourself by doing Tai Chi incorrectly. This is ridiculous! My teacher has always said "if it is not healthy for your body it is not Tai Chi." Tai Chi means perfect balance. If you practice Tai Chi with an imbalance in your waist , legs, upper torso or head you can do harm to your body.

All of these subtle nuances in the legs, waist, shoulders, elbows and fingers are there for the purpose of maintaining energy in your structure throughout the entire span of the movement. Fighting is completely unpredictable. What if you are attacking with a Brush Knee and your opponent is previous to your attack and catches you at "bru" or at "sh" or even at "kn"? Will your frame crumble? Will your footwork be rooted and solid even before you reach the full extention of the posture? Does your advance contain the element of retreat?

Will you be able to change in a fraction of a second and turn the situation back to your advantage?

Maintaining structure and alignment helps to maintain energy in the whole body. Keeping this energy constant prevents your opponent from finding an advantage because there will be no variance in energy levels for your opponent to interpret. Attaining to the level of interpreting energy is the second of your two goals in Tai Chi. Wu Yu Qing said, "Get to know the opponent but do not reveal yourself to him."

Another important advantage for fighting that is developed from practicing these structural alignment principles is the elimination of the effect of reaction force on your frame. You know, of course, Newton's Third Law of Motion states that for every action there is an equal and opposite reaction. Being equal and opposite, it immediately effects the power of your strike. Certainly, you cannot stop the Laws of physics from applying to you but by mastering these principles of alignment you will be able to use Newton's Law to your advantage. Reaction force can reduce the effectiveness of your strike by imbalancing you but only if your frame is not structurally sound. By creating a Chuan Jia (fighting frame) that is structurally perfect and full of Jing you can neutralize the effect reaction force has on your striking power. In fact, reaction force can actually increase your striking power by rooting you deeper into the earth if your Chuan

Jia (fighting frame) is correct and properly energized throughout. Yes, this is very difficult. Tai Chi truly takes a lifetime to master. The Treatise on Tai Chi Chuan by Wang Tsung-Yueh states that "without long practice one will not suddenly understand Tai Chi Chuan." There is another Chinese proverb that is worth quoting here, "Practicing without effort, is effort wasted in the end and when you are old it will be too late."

The Test of the Eight Stabilities

The Test of the Eight Stabilities

The Eight Stabilities test, also known as "Jing Testing", refers to testing the Chuan Jia (Fighting Frame) of a student by applying force to each of the Eight Gates in order to determine if the structural integrity of the posture is sound. This test is of paramount importance to all serious practitioners of Tai Chi and should be performed on each and every posture in the 108 movement form (yes, even the one-legged ones).

You should start by testing your students in only one direction - from the front or directly against the energy of the strike. For example, have your student perform a brush knee posture and then place your hand against the edge of his palm and apply force directly back down his arm. If he remains still, great...if not, then make correction to his frame where necessary and test again. Repeat this process over and over, having your student change sides when he tires, until he is able to remain still without applying more force back at you (resisting). In order to insure that he is not resisting, randomly release your force and see if he falls forward.

As your students progress, begin to test the other two forward corners in the same manner (applying force to the torso) and then moving to the three rear directions and finally to the two lateral sides.

When testing, do not use quick, explosive force. Start with just a touch and gradually build your force against the spot where you are testing. This will give your beginner students time to come to an understanding about how the structure of their frame relates to the force you are applying. When, while testing, you find problems with your students' frames, look first to the waist and legs for correction. This is where you will find the major problems according to Yang Cheng-Fu.

Here you will see how to Jing test a few different postures.

As you improve you may need more people to test you.

Here you see the Eight Stabilities Test below

You will test all four sides and four corners for each posture

Section Four

Strength
and
Flexibility

緊緊

和弱點

Tightness and Weakness

In order to perform the Tai Chi postures correctly you must have both strength and flexibility, especially in the legs and waist. If you have read this text through to this section then this fact is already very obvious to you. Where there is inflexibility (tightness) there is weakness. Where there is weakness there is the opportunity for an opponent to take advantage of you. No, Tai Chi is not about the strong overcoming the weak but it is about you being the master of your body. How can you say that you are the master of your body when you cannot make it perform the tasks that you ask of it. Without maintenance of flexibility over time the human body shrinks and range of motion becomes more and more limited. Anything that decreases your range of motion subtracts years from your life. Increasing your range of motion enhances strength, adds comfort to everyday activities and lengthens your life and the enjoyment of that life. Tight or weak muscles in the waist and legs can cause improper structural alignment, poor transitioning between Substantial and Insubstantial and incontinuity of movement. Flexibility eases the flow of Qi and blood thoughout the body thereby encreasing overall health. Flexibility also enhances speed. Yang Cheng-Fu was known to say "sometimes you have to block." He meant that sometimes things can happen so quickly and so unpredctably that you cannot be previous to the attack. A little extra speed is helpful in these situations.

Increasing your speed has a very fortunate by-product; an increase in striking power. According to the second of the five physical laws of motion; energy = 1/2 x mass x velocity squared (e = 1/2mv2). If you are implementing the concepts in this book and have your upper and lower parts coordinated then (and only then) is your mass a constant in this equation. Since you cannot increase your mass the only way to increase energy is to increase speed. Of course, the state of being *Song* does increase speed significantly by eliminating hindrances caused by muscle tension. Increasing flexibility and lengthening your range of motion allows you to reach farther with greater ease. A proverb that is quoted quite often in Chinese martial arts is "inch long, inch strong" meaning that the ability to reach longer increases your power.

Exercises To Improve Your Tai Chi

Here are a few of the exercises that I have students perform if they have a problem with weakness or inflexibility in certain areas. I am very fond of exercises that can be done in a doorway because I have found that very few of my students are without one (so they cannot give me an excuse for not doing the execise at home). I have yet to find a student who did not need the exercise for Snake Creeps Down posture.

Snake Creeps Down

Stand in a doorway with the toes of the Substantial foot pointed at the corner of the doorway. Hold on to the door facing with your "whip" hand and squat into Snake Creeps Down being diligent to implement all of the Jings and to keep the spine straight. Lift up. Squat down again. When you tire rest and change legs.

Your Achilles Heel

Stand inside a doorway facing the lock side. Grab the door facing on both sides with your hands and lift the toes of one foot and place the heel as close to the door facing as possible. Begin to pull your chest toward the door facing as you stand as tall as possible. You should feel the stretching sensation in your achilles tendon. The flexibility of the Achilles tendon facilitates the inner rotation of the Insubstantial thigh in the Gong Bu by enhancing your ability to turn your rear foot inwardly.

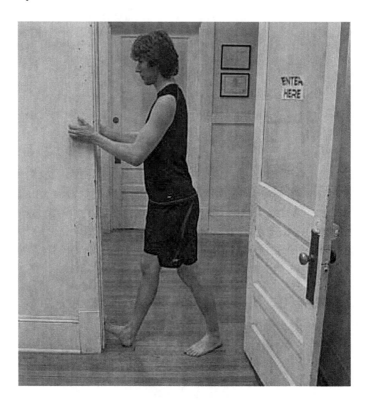

Square Horse

Sometimes called Horse Sitting. This exercise is a great overall workout for the legs and waist. You should concentrate on rotating both thighs inwardly and then countering that action with an outer rotation on the shins. Make certain that the tailbone is scooped enough for the spine to be straight and breath deeply. Press the ouside of the knees against the inside of the doorway and move the ankle bones toward the center slightly to create the opening in the Gwa. Hold on to the door facing until you are strong enough to release it.

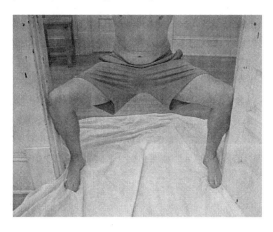

Head to Knee Stretch

I actually like to call this stretch "head beyond the knee." Keep the spine straight and the crown of the head lengthening away from the tailbone. Do not scoop the tailbone ... in fact, do the opposite of scooping the tailbone (counter-nutation of the sacrum to activate the origins of the biceps femoris, the abductors and the adductors of the thigh). Use a belt or strap until you can grab your toes and still keep the spine straight.

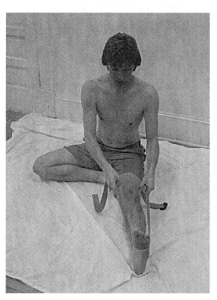
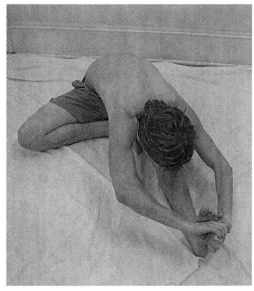

Seated Forward Bend

This stretch is excellent for lengthening everything from the back of your heels to the back of your neck (in sanskrit it is called *paschimottanasana* or the extreme western stretch - the west side of your body being the back). Lengthen the spine and counter-nutate the sacrum. Use a belt or strap until you can grab your toes while keeping the spine straight. Flex the toes of both feet back toward your nose to activate the insertion of the biceps femoris of the thigh and the origins of the gastrocnemius and soleus muscles of the calves.

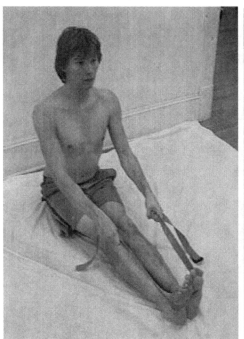 

Cobbler's Stretch

Great stretch for the hips, abductors and lower back. Spine straight, counter-nutate the sacrum and move the lower belly toward the heels to feel the stretch. To facilitate the opening of the hips turn the bottoms of your feet open as though they were a book your were reading.

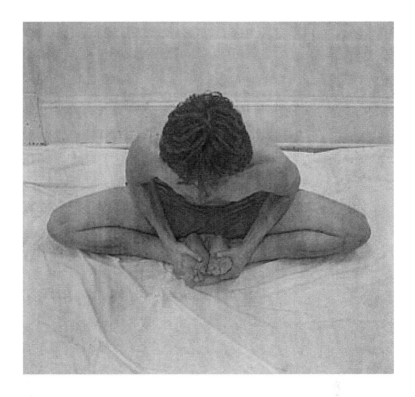

Night and Day Stretch

Very good stretch for the hamstrings and lower back. This stretch can be performed anywhere you can prop one leg up; the back of a chair, in a window sill or on the hood of your car. I also have my students practice lifting their heel off of whatever they are propped up on in order to strengthen the hip flexors thereby enhancing the kicking postures.

References

I recommend reading as many different translations of the Chinese texts as you can find. It is always helpful to get several different translators and practitioners' insights. This list is also my recommended reading list and is in no particular order.

Lost T'ai-chi Classics from the Late Ch'ing Dynasty by Douglas Wile

Tai Chi Touchstones: Yang Family Secret Transmissions by Douglas Wile

Mastering Yang Style Taijiquan by Fu Zhongwen

Tai Chi Chuan's Internal Secrets by Doc-Fai Wong and Jane Hallander

Power of Internal Martial Arts: Combat Secrets of Ba Gua, Tai Chi, and Hsing-I by Bruce Frantzis

Art of War by Sun Tzu

A Book of Five Rings by Miyamoto Musashi

Anatomy of Movement by Blandine Calais-Germain

Tai Chi Secrets of the Yang Style by Dr. Yang Jwing-Ming

Somatics - Reawakening the Mind's Control of Movement, Flexibility, and Health by Thomas Hanna

Tai Chi's Ancestors: the Making of an Internal Art by Douglas Wile

Cheng-Tzu's Thirteen Treatises on T'ai Chi Ch'uan by Cheng Man Ch'Ing

Demystifying Tai Chi Chuan by Tu-Ky Lam

T'ai Chi Ch'uan Ta Wen: Questions and Answers on T'ai Chi Ch'uan by Chen Wei-Ming, Benjamin Pang Jeng Lo, and Robert W. Smith

Ultimate Guide To Tai Chi : The Best of Inside Kung-Fu by John R. Little and Curtis Wong

There Are No Secrets: Professor Cheng Man Ch'ing and His T'ai Chi Chuan by Wolfe Lowenthal

T'ai Chi: The "Supreme Ultimate" Exercise For Health, Sport And

Self-defense by Cheng Man-Ch'Ing and Robert W. Smith

Tao and Longevity: Mind-Body Transformation by Huai-Chin Nan translated by Wen Kuan Chu, Ph.D

Taoist Health Exercise Book by Da Liu

Living Qi Gong by John Alton

The Essence of Tai Chi Chuan: The Literary Tradition by Benjamin P. Lo, Martin Inn, Susan Foe and Robert Amacker

T'ai Chi Classics by Waysun Liao

T'ai Chi Boxing Chronicle by Kuo Lien-Ying and Guttman

The Essence and Applications of Taijiquan by Yang Cheng-fu Translated by Louis Swaim

About the Author

Steffan de Graffenried is a linguist and martial arts instructor currently residing in Alabama, USA. He has been studying the martial arts since 1972. He has had the opportunity to study myriad of martial systems over the years including Judo, Tang Soo Do, Tae Kwon Do, Iaido, Kenjutsu, Aikido, Hung Gar, Northern Shaolin, Seven Star Mantis, Bagua, Hsing I, Choy Li Fut and Yang Family Tai Chi Chuan. His current teacher is Grandmaster Doc-Fai Wong a fifth generation grandmaster of Yang Family Tai Chi Chuan and Choy Li Fut kung fu. He began his study of Yang Family Tai Chi Chuan in 1992 with Grandmaster Wong and quickly became infatuated with its complexities and its subtleties. Mr. de Graffenried is available for workshops and may be contacted at anatomyoftaichi@gmail.com.

Printed in the United States
114445LV00006B/31-36/P